THE LITTLE BROWN EGG BOOK

Appetizing recipes using nature's most versatile food.

In the same series
THE LITTLE BROWN BEAN BOOK
THE LITTLE BROWN BREAD BOOK
THE LITTLE BROWN RICE BOOK

THE LITTLE BROWN EGG BOOK

by

David Eno

Illustrated by Clive Birch

THORSONS PUBLISHERS LIMITED
Wellingborough, Northamptonshire

This enlarged, revised and reset edition first published
1983
Second Impression 1984

© THORSONS PUBLISHERS LTD 1983

British Library Cataloguing in Publication Data

Eno, David
    The little brown egg book.
    1. Cookery (Eggs)
    I. Title
    641.6'75   TX745

    ISBN 0-7225-0851-4

Printed and bound in Great Britain

CONTENTS

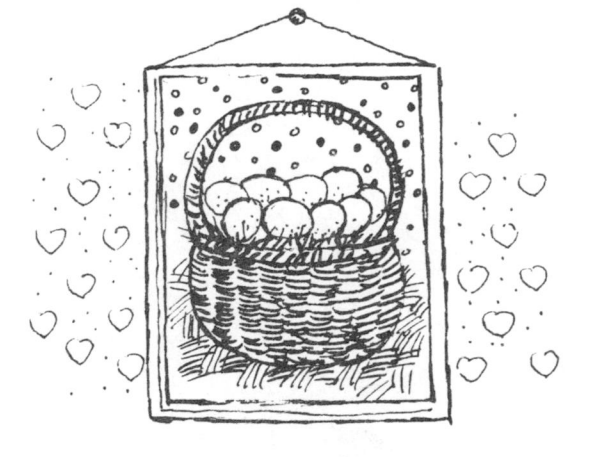

INTRODUCTION

Eggs are a concentrated food and a particularly good source of protein. The various amino acids of which protein is composed are all present in almost exactly the quantities which the body can utilize most effectively. Over 90 per cent of protein present in eggs can be utilized compared with 68 per cent in meat and 45 per cent in peanuts. Apart from protein, eggs contain useful amounts of vitamins A and D, Iron and Riboflavin.

Although eggs have been listed among foods containing saturated animal fat, which can contribute to hardening of the arteries, they only contain 12 per cent as compared to meat which may contain up to 50 per cent fat, and butter which contains 82 per cent.

EGGS IN COOKERY

Not only are eggs nutritionally valuable, but they possess many other useful qualities. They help to bind dry mixtures, they form an impervious coating for frying, they increase the tenacity of dough retaining air and increasing lightness. Egg yolk can be used to emulsify oil which is useful in mayonnaise and sauces, and lastly, eggs add colour and flavour to all dishes.

The longer eggs are cooked the more indigestible they become although this is less so when they are cooked in a mixture. The whites of hard boiled eggs are the most difficult to digest.

SUPERMARKET EGGS

All eggs on sale in shops and supermarkets unless expressly marked otherwise are obtained from battery hens, which are kept two or three to a cage in vast factory like buildings, leading a thoroughly miserable existence. It is mainly for this reason that I strongly recommend the avoidance of battery eggs.

FREE-RANGE EGGS!

Free-range hens are allowed to roam where they can obtain sun, air, and natural foods to supplement their diet. Free-range eggs though more expensive are infinitely preferable to battery eggs. They are strong shelled, with richly coloured and flavoured yolks. By buying free-range eggs you can be sure of avoiding antibiotics and chemicals which may be present in battery eggs, and because they are usually produced locally they are fresher than battery eggs which can be ten to fourteen days old.

FARM EGGS

This term rarely denotes free-range eggs. They are more likely to be battery eggs sold directly from farm to shop. Many shopkeepers are confused about the difference between fresh eggs, farm eggs and free-range eggs, so choose your source carefully.

There is no difference between the contents of brown and white eggs. Some breeds of hen lay white eggs, others brown.

TESTING FOR FRESHNESS

Place the suspect egg in a tumbler containing cold water with one teaspoonful of sea salt added. One of the following should happen:

1. If it rests on the bottom it is fresh.

2. If it stands on end it is a week or so old.

3. If it floats with part of the shell above the water it is stale.

SEASONING FOR EGGS

Seasonings should complement the natural taste of a dish, not hide it. Be careful not to over-season.

Sea salt: contains many trace elements, each important in its own way for the correct functioning of the body. Heavily processed foods often lack these vital elements.

Pepper: always use freshly ground black peppercorns. Their hot spicy flavour is worlds apart from the usual lifeless grey powder.

HERBS

Many herbs bring out the flavour of eggs particularly well and I always make a point of using plenty of fresh herbs in egg dishes and as a garnish.

Try some of the following:

Basil, Bay, Chervil, Chives, Dill, Garlic, Lovage, Marigold, Marjoram, Mint, Nasturtium leaves, Sorrel, Parsley, Rosemary, Sage, Salad Burnet, Summer Savory, Tarragon, Thyme.

SNACKS

CODDLED EGG

Boil a pan of water. Remove from the heat, pop in the egg and leave for 10 minutes. The white will be soft and creamy and more digestible than an ordinary boiled egg.

SCRAMBLED EGGS

½ oz (15g) butter or olive oil
2 eggs
1½ tablespoonsful milk
Freshly ground black pepper and sea salt

1. Melt the butter in a pan over a low heat.

2. Beat the eggs lightly with the milk in a bowl and season to taste.

3. Pour into the pan and continue to use a low heat, stirring all the time with a wooden spatula. Remove from the heat before it has quite set and serve immediately.

Variations:
  (a) Add a little grated cheese or yeast extract or both.

  (b) Add fried mushrooms with a little chopped parsley.

  (c) Try cream cheese stirred slowly into the cooked eggs with a touch of garlic.

  (d) Serve with hot buttered spinach and lightly grilled tomatoes.

BEATEN EGG SOUP

2 pints (1 litre) vegetable stock
1 tablespoonful tomato purée
1 tablespoonful yeast extract
4 eggs
1½ tablespoonsful wholemeal flour
3 tablespoonsful finely chopped herbs
Seasoning to taste

1. Heat up the stock and dissolve the tomato purée and yeast extract in it.

2. Beat the eggs, blending in the flour, and when the stock is simmering slowly dribble in the egg mixture.

3. Keep stirring the soup and thin strands of egg will coagulate to form a noodle like substance. Serve sprinkled with chopped herbs and season.

EGG SPREAD WITH OLIVES

2 oz (50g) butter
2 teaspoonsful mayonnaise
2 oz (50g) hard boiled eggs, chopped
4 oz (100g) olives
1 tablespoonful chopped parsley

Soften the butter and blend into the other ingredients. Serve on crackers, ryebread, or in sandwiches.

EGG BASKETS

This is a most attractive starter or snack which will amuse and tempt children and adults alike.

3 eggs
2 oz (50g) mushrooms
1 oz (25g) butter or vegetable margarine
Sea salt
Freshly ground pepper
Bunch fresh parsley

1. Hard boil the eggs.

2. Finely chop or mince the mushrooms and fry them in the butter.

3. When the eggs are done remove the shells under cold water and cut in half lengthways. Keep the whites warm. Remove the yolks and mash with the mushrooms and seasoning.

4. Re-fill the whites with this mixture and garnish with a sprig of parsley. Stick parsley stems into the egg to make a handle for the basket.

STUFFED EGGS

Hard boil the eggs and cut across lengthways.
Remove the yolk and pound with butter, sea salt,
cayenne, lemon juice, grated cheese, chopped fried
mushroom, or any tasty morsel. Pile back into the
yolk cavity and decorate with herbs, pimento,
olives, etc., and serve on a croûton of toast spread
with the filling.

DRESSINGS

MAYONNAISE

---

1 egg yolk
*2 to 4 teaspoonsful wine vinegar or lemon
juice*
*½ pint (250ml) vegetable oil (preferably
olive or salad quality)*
½ teaspoonful clear honey
½ clove of garlic
*Freshly ground black pepper and sea salt to
taste*

All the ingredients should be at room temperature.

1. Whisk the egg yolk in a bowl or beat with a fork, adding a little of the vinegar or lemon juice.

2. Begin adding the oil drop by drop beating furiously until thickening is detected. Continue to beat now adding the oil in a slow trickle.

3. When all the oil is added, which takes at least 5 minutes by hand, add the rest of the ingredients and mix well.

Note: If the oil is added too quickly or if the bowl is not really clean the oil will separate into globules, and beat as you may will not revert to a thick creamy texture. If this happens all is not lost. Begin again with a clean bowl and fresh egg yolk adding the separated mixture drop by drop as if it were the oil. Prevention is better than cure so always proceed very slowly and patiently in the initial stages.

To keep the mayonnaise store in a screw topped jar in the fridge. As it has no artificial preservatives it will only keep for about 5 days. Now you have your mayonnaise here are some delicious excuses for eating it: Fresh boiled asparagus tips, globe artichokes, raw or boiled cauliflower, with plenty of greens, all manner of salads, vegetable pies, fennel, boiled eggs, watercress, french beans, peas, carrots, boiled rice, corn on the cob, etc.

AILLOLI

Ailloli is made with the reckless addition of more garlic to the above recipe. For best effect add as much as you or your guests can take. Start the bidding at two cloves! In Provence a dish called ailloli garni is made. This is a sparkling array of fish, raw and cooked vegetables of every kind, including the occasional snail and a huge bowl of ailloli. With the addition of French crusty bread the feast can begin! (The fish and snails may be omitted!)

AILLAIDE

To the basic mayonnaise add garlic crushed in a mortar with a few grilled and skinned hazelnuts and a few walnuts. These are best skinned by soaking in boiling water for 1 minute.

AVOCADO EGG MAYONNAISE

Use the basic mayonnaise described earlier. When blended with the avocado it produces the most delightfully cool green dressing for the eggs.

4 eggs
1 ripe avocado
½ teaspoonful lemon juice
4 tablespoonsful basic mayonnaise (or good quality bought mayonnaise)
4 tablespoonsful natural yogurt
Ground sea salt
Paprika

1. Hard boil the eggs and cool them under running water.

2. While the eggs are boiling halve the avocado longways and remove the stone. Place one of the halves in a liquidizer or food processor together with the lemon juice, mayonnaise, yogurt and sea salt to taste. Liquidize until smooth.

3. Shell the eggs and cut them in half longways. Lay them out on a dish, cut-side downwards, and pour over the dressing.

4. Use the other half of the avocado, sliced thinly, crossways, to garnish the edge of the dish. Sprinkle with paprika. An alternative

method of serving is to slice the eggs and avocado straight into glasses and pour over the dressing as before.

GREEN MAYONNAISE

Choose a selection of fresh herbs and a few leaves of spinach. Blanch for 2 minutes in boiling water and pound to a paste with a mortar and pestle. Blend into the basic mayonnaise mixture.

CLIVE BIRLH

LIGHT MEALS

HAWAIIAN SALAD

4 hard-boiled eggs
1 cupful cooked brown rice
1 cupful hot mashed potato
½ cupful French dressing
Sea salt
Freshly ground pepper
1 tablespoonful green pepper, chopped
1 tablespoonful onion, chopped
1 tablespoonful fresh parsley, chopped
2 tablespoonsful pimento, chopped

1. Liquidize the hard-boiled eggs and mix with the rice and hot mashed potato.

2. Stir in the French dressing and season to taste. Chill and just before serving add the rest of the ingredients.

3. Slice the remaining eggs and use as a garnish with a few sprigs of parsley on top.

TOMATO EGGS

4 large tomatoes
Cayenne pepper
Sea salt
1½ oz (40g) butter
2 eggs
1 tablespoonful chopped parsley

1. Cut the tomatoes in half and remove the pulp. Lay out on a greased tin, add seasoning and a small piece of butter to each, cover with a piece of greaseproof paper and cook at 375°F/190°C (Gas Mark 5) for 15 minutes.

2. Using a liquidizer blend the eggs and tomato pulp then add the chopped parsley and season to taste.

3. Melt the butter in a saucepan and gently cook the egg mixture until it sets. Spoon into the tomato cases and garnish with chopped parsley.

CREAMED EGGS AND MUSHROOMS

1½ oz (40g) butter
1 tablespoonful fresh lemon juice
½ lb (250g) mushrooms
1 tablespoonful fresh parsley, chopped
½ tablespoonful fresh chives, chopped
4 large eggs
Sea salt and freshly ground pepper
4 tablespoonsful double cream

1. Pre-heat the oven to 350°F/180°C (Gas Mark 4).

2. Melt the butter in a frying pan and add the lemon juice. *Sauté* the chopped mushrooms until they are cooked then turn off the heat and stir in the chopped parsley and chives.

3. Divide this between 4 small individual dishes. Break an egg into each dish and season to taste. Top with the cream and bake until set. Serve straight away.

EGGS ROMAINE

½ lb (250g) fresh spinach
1½ oz (40g) butter
½ clove garlic
Sea salt
Freshly ground pepper
Grated nutmeg
4 large eggs
2 oz (50g) Parmesan or any cheese preferred,
grated

1. Wash the spinach and cook over a gentle heat in a closed pan with no added water for 10 to 15 minutes.

2. When the spinach is cooked drain and mash with the butter and a touch of garlic. Season with sea salt, freshly ground black pepper and grated nutmeg.

3. Divide the spinach between 4 individual ovenproof dishes and make a hollow in the centre of each. Into each break an egg and top with grated cheese. Grill for 5 to 10 minutes so that the eggs are set and the cheese lightly browned. Serve straight away.

POACHED EGGS ON POTATO CAKES

½ lb (250g) wholemeal flour
1 lb (500g) mashed potato
Sea salt
Freshly ground pepper
1 egg
Butter and 1 egg per person

1. Mix the flour, potato and seasoning then add the egg. Knead together roll out on a floured board to about ½ inch (1cm) thick.

2. Cut out with a glass or biscuit cutter and bake on a greased tray at 375°F/190°C (Gas Mark 5) for 20 minutes. Split open and serve buttered with a poached egg on top. Garnish with parsley.

CREAM CHEESE QUICHE

½ lb (250g) wholemeal short crust pastry
3 oz (75g) Gruyère or Cheddar cheese
3 oz (75g) cream cheese
3 eggs
3 spring onions
Sea salt
Freshly ground pepper
Freshly ground nutmeg
Garlic

1. Pre-heat the oven to 400°F/200°C (Gas Mark 6).

2. Line an 8 inch (20cm) flan tin with the pastry and bake blind for 10 to 15 minutes.

3. Grate the Gruyère and mix with the cream cheese.

4. Beat the eggs and finely chop the onions.

5. Mix all the ingredients together and season to taste adding a little garlic if liked.

6. Turn into the pastry case and bake for 20 to 25 minutes when the top should be brown. Serve hot or cold with salad and baked potatoes.

BAKED EGG POTATOES

4 large potatoes
4 eggs
1 oz (25g) polyunsaturated margarine
2 tablespoonsful milk or cream
Sea salt and freshly ground pepper

1. Scrub and prepare the potatoes. Mark a line on the skin with the point of a knife where the top will later be cut to make a lid. Bake at 375°F/190°C (Gas Mark 5) oven until done.

2. Remove the lids and scoop the potato out of both halves. Mash the potato with the margarine, milk and seasoning until smooth. Half fill each bottom shell with the mashed potato then break and egg on top. Add a teaspoonful of milk to each potato, cover with the lid and return to the oven for 15 minutes.

3. Remove from the oven and discard the lids. Pipe the remaining mashed potato on top, lightly brown under the grill and serve at once. These potatoes make a good tea-time snack, or can be served as part of a main meal with salad etc.

EGG AND CARROT BAKE

For a light lunch or an appetizing snack at any time of the day.

> *¾ lb (350g) carrots*
> *½ onion*
> *1 oz (25g) butter*
> *Sea salt*
> *Freshly grated nutmeg*
> *Freshly ground black pepper*
> *2 large eggs*
> *2 tablespoonsful milk*
> *1 tablespoonful chives, chopped*
> *2 slices wholemeal bread*
> *1 tablespoonful basic mayonnaise*

1. Pre-heat the oven to 400°F/200°C (Gas Mark 6).

2. Grate the carrot and onion and fry in the butter until soft. Season with sea salt, nutmeg and freshly ground black pepper to taste then place in the bottom of a greased ½ pint (250ml) ovenproof dish.

3. Beat the egg with the milk and chopped chives and pour into the dish.

4. Spread the bread with mayonnaise and cut into 1 inch (2.5cm) squares. Arrange on top

of the dish, mayonnaise side up. Place on the
middle shelf of the oven and bake for 20 to
25 minutes, when the egg should have set all
the way through and the bread browned.
Serve straight away. A side salad makes a
good accompaniment.

CAULIFLOWER CHEESE BAKE

1 medium cauliflower
1 oz (25g) butter or polyunsaturated
margarine
4 oz (100g) Cheddar cheese
Sea salt
Freshly ground pepper
4 eggs

1. Steam or boil the cauliflower for 15 minutes. Drain and chop into small pieces then return to the pan and stir in the butter.

2. Take a greased oven-proof dish and make alternate layers of cauliflower and grated cheese adding a little seasoning to each layer. The final layer should be cheese and onto this break the eggs. Bake for 20 minutes at 375°F/190°C (Gas Mark 5) and serve. Grilled tomatoes go well with this dish.

OMELETTES

MAKING AN OMELETTE

Always use fresh eggs and be prepared to serve immediately after cooking. Set the pan heating with 1 teaspoonful of oil or preferably butter. Beat the eggs well with a fork adding the seasoning and any desired herbs. When the butter or oil is hot enough to begin smoking pour in the beaten eggs. Keep lifting the edge of the omelette with a fork to allow more liquid from the top to run under and set. Add any filling and continue to cook until the underside begins to brown.

If you have used a sufficiently hot pan the omelette should have risen somewhat, but if not this can always be encouraged by putting under a hot grill for a few moments. When the cooking is finished loosen the edges if stuck, fold in half and serve.

Garnish with thin slices of tomato, cress, lettuce, herbs, etc. The entire process should only take about 3 minutes so is excellent for lunchtime snacks. For a very light omelette separate the whites and beat separately until frothy then fold in the yolks and seasoning and proceed as before.

Note: Omelettes are so versatile and quick to prepare that they ought to be served often. They make an ideal light lunch, but don't forget to garnish with slices tomato, lettuce, parsley, sliced onion rings etc. For a change try more unusual garnishes such as endives, chicory, slices of red and green pepper, and fennel. A slice or two of good wholemeal bread completes the meal.

Don't be put off by the problem of serving omelettes to several people at once. Buy two omelette pans. Get everything ready before the meal. For ordinary omelettes have the eggs for each portion ready beaten in a separate cup. For souffle omelettes prepare the mixture in one large batch then divide into separate cups. Have any filling ready prepared, and also the garnish. Enlist an assistant to take the omelettes to the table, and begin, cooking two at a time.

HERB OMELETTE

Add a tablespoonful of finely chopped fresh herbs such as basil, parsley, thyme, chives, marjoram. A little chopped onion or shallot can also be added.

CHEESE OMELETTE

Gruyère is the best cheese for this purpose although a strongly flavoured Cheddar is quite suitable. Grate a couple of ounces into the centre of the omelette before folding. Use plenty of seasoning.

MUSHROOM AND CREAM CHEESE OMELETTE

Chop and fry a few large mushrooms. Spread a layer of cream cheese over the partially cooked omelette. Add the mushrooms with extra seasoning then fold and cook for one minute more. Try serving with pumpernickel or any rye bread.

TOMATO OMELETTE

Fill the omelette with a layer of very thinly sliced tomatoes sprinkled with sea salt and freshly ground pepper and a good tablespoonful of freshly chopped basil. Top with more sliced tomato and a basil leaf.

SPANISH OMELETTE

This recipe is ideal for using up cooked potato and any other left over vegetables. It takes only about 5 minutes to cook and when ready it should be served immediately so have everything else ready prepared, and pre-heat the grill which will be needed for the last stage of cooking.

> 5 large eggs
> 3 or 4 medium boiled potatoes
> 1 onion
> 1 green or red pepper
> 1 cupful cooked vegetables

1. Prepare the cooked vegetables by dicing or slicing and lightly fry any raw ingredients such as onion or peppers.

2. Heat the pan and beat up the eggs as in the previous recipe. Pour half of the eggs into the pan and cook for a minute or 2.

3. Add the filling in a layer and cover with the rest of the eggs. Continue to cook under the grill until the eggs have risen and turned golden. Sprinkle with a few chopped chives or other herbs before serving. Serves 4.

BASIC SOUFFLÉ OMELETTE

2 eggs
2 tablespoonsful hot water
Sea salt
Freshly ground pepper
¼ oz (7g) butter

1. Pre-heat the grill.

2. Separate the whites of the eggs and whisk until stiff.

3. Beat the yolks and add the hot water and seasoning. Beat again and when thoroughly blended fold in the whites.

4. Melt the butter allowing it to coat the pan all over. Pour in the mixture and cook over a moderate heat until the bottom begins to brown.

5. Now place under the grill and when the top is set, but before it browns, remove and make a cut across the centre. Loosen the sides and fold in half. Turn onto a hot plate and serve straight away.

SAVOURY SOUFFLÉ OMELETTES

Any of the additions for normal omelettes can be used with the recipe above. For example make a cheese souffle omelette by sprinkling the top of the basic omelette with 2 oz (50g) of grated cheese during the final cooking under the grill.

PARSLEY SOUFFLÉ OMELETTE

Add two tablespoonsful of fresh chopped parsley to the egg yolks before the white is added.

SOUFFLÉS

SOUFFLÉ

Basic Recipe
  1 oz (25g) 81% wholemeal flour
  3 to 4 eggs
  2 oz (50g) polyunsaturated margarine or
  butter
  ½ pint (250ml) milk
  4 to 8 oz (100-250g) cooked puréed fruit plus
  sweetening for a sweet soufflé

or

  4 to 8 oz (100-250g) vegetables or cheese
  plus herbs and seasoning for a savoury
  soufflé

1. Melt the fat and stir in the flour, cooking
    gently but not browning.

2. Remove from the heat and stir in the milk.
    When smooth cook over a low heat until the
    mixture leaves the sides of the pan clean.

3. Separate the egg whites from the yolks,
    adding the yolks one at a time to the mixture
    and stirring well. Add the rest of the
    ingredients and the seasoning or sweetening.

4. Fold the stiffly beaten whites into the mixture

with a metal spoon and pour into a greased oven proof dish, allowing room for a doubling in size.

5.   Bake at 350°F/180°C (Gas Mark 4) for 45 minutes or until risen and browned on top. Do not open the oven for the first 30 minutes or the soufflé will sink. Serve immediately from the oven.

CHEESE SOUFFLÉ

Follow the basic recipe adding:
 3 to 4 oz (75-100g) strong flavoured cheese,
 grated
 ½ teaspoonful yeast extract
 Grated nutmeg to taste

SPANISH SOUFFLÉ

Follow the basic recipe adding:
 1 small onion
 1 small green pepper
 1 tomato
 All chopped and fried in a little oil

CHESTNUT SOUFFLÉ (SWEET)

Add to the basic recipe:
*   4 tablespoonsful chestnut purée*
*   Honey to sweeten*
*   Pinch of sea salt*

SWEETS

CHOCOLATE MOUSSE

---

4 oz (100g) plain chocolate
4 eggs
¼ pint (150ml) double cream

Break up the chocolate and place in a bowl over hot water. When melted stir in the separated egg yolks then fold in the stiffly beaten whites. Pour into individual glasses and chill to set. Top with dollops of cream.

FRIARS OMELETTES

6 cooking apples
2 oz (50g) cane sugar
2 oz (50g) butter
2 eggs
2 cupsful wholemeal breadcrumbs
Honey

1. Prepare and cook the apples as for apple sauce, stirring in the sugar and butter. Allow to cool completely and fold in the well beaten eggs.

2. Oil an ovenproof dish or casserole and sprinkle the bottom with the breadcrumbs. Cover with the apples and top with another layer of breadcrumbs. Bake at 350°F/180°C (Gas Mark 4) for 35 minutes and serve topped with honey.

CREAM FRITTERS

4 eggs
4 tablespoonsful honey
1 pint (500ml) cream
Pinch cinnamon and ginger
1 cupful wholemeal breadcrumbs
1 orange

1. Beat the eggs and blend with the honey, cream, and spices.

2. Beat in enough breadcrumbs to make a thick batter. Drop small quantities of this into hot oil and fry. Serve with a squeeze of fresh orange juice.

FRENCH PROMISES

½ pint (250ml) milk
2 teaspoonsful French brandy
1 egg
Pinch ground ginger
Wholemeal flour
Demerara sugar

1. Mix the milk, brandy, egg and a pinch of ginger.

2. Beat in the flour until a thick creamy consistency is achieved then fry dollops in a hot frying pan. Turn when golden and cook the other side. Sprinkle with sugar and serve.

EGG CUSTARD

2 to 4 eggs
1 pink (500ml) milk
1½ oz (25-40g) cane sugar

1. Warm the milk to blood heat and dissolve the sugar in it.

2. Beat the eggs thoroughly then add the milk and beat again until completely mixed. To cook, stand the bowl in a pan of water and simmer gently until thickened. Overcooking will cause curdling.

APPLE CAKE WITH EGGS

2 eggs
4 oz (100g) butter
¾ lb (350g) wholemeal flour
1½ teaspoonsful baking powder
½ teaspoonful ground sea salt
½ teaspoonful ground ginger
4 oz (100g) soft brown sugar
1½ cupsful grated cooking apple

1. Separate the egg yolks and whites and beat separately.

2. Cream the butter and sugar together and stir in the yolks.

3. Sift the dry ingredients together and add gradually to the mixture beating well.

4. Grate the apples and fold them together with the egg whites into the mixture.

5. Place in an oiled shallow cake tin lined with greaseproof paper and bake at 375°F/190°C (Gas Mark 5) for 1 hour. Can be served hot or cold.

LEMON CURD

This is the real thing, and can become addictive! As it doesn't keep for long it's best to make it in small batches.

6 eggs
4 oz (100g) butter or polyunsaturated margarine
1 lb (500g) Demerara sugar
Juice and rind of 4 lemons

1. Using a double boiler, or large basin over a pan of boiling water, melt the butter and add the lemon juice, sugar and finely grated rind. Stir until the mixture is smooth.

2. Thoroughly beat the eggs and stir into the pan. Keep stirring until it thickens.

3. Pour into pre-heated, sterilized jars, seal and leave to cool. Sealed jars will last up to 12 weeks, opened jars should be kept in the fridge and eaten within 10 days.

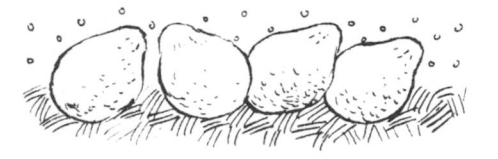

BLACKCURRANT SORBET

1 lb (500g) blackcurrants
½ lb (250g) Demerara sugar
Water
2 large egg whites
4 oz (100g) double cream

1. Prepare and wash the blackcurrants. Add the sugar and just enough water to cover in a saucepan. Bring to the boil over a gentle heat and simmer until the juice runs.

2. Sieve the fruit pulp and freeze in a shallow container for 2 to 4 hours until half frozen. Remove and break up the solid portions with a fork.

3. Whisk the egg whites until stiff and fold into the syrup with a metal spoon. Return to the freezer for a further 2 to 4 hours until firm. Before serving allow the sorbet to soften at room temperature for 15 minutes. Serve with whipped cream.

DRINKS

EGG NOG

1 tablespoonful sherry or brandy
1 tablespoonful single cream
Honey to sweeten
1 egg white

Put the brandy into a glass and add the cream and a little honey to taste and mix well. Whisk the egg white to a thick froth and stir lightly into the glass.

HOT EGG NOG

1 egg yolk
1 pint (500ml) milk
1 tablespoonful honey
1 tablespoonful whiskey or brandy

1. Beat together the egg yolk and the honey then stir in the spirit.

2. Bring the milk to the boil and pour over the mixed ingredients. Stir well and serve.

51

EGG AND WINE

1 glass port or sherry
1 egg
1 glass boiling water
1 teaspoonful honey

Beat the egg well in a cup with the honey. When dissolved add the hot water and then the wine. Strain and serve.

EGG FLIP

5 eggs
3 pints (1.5 litres) ale
3 oz (75g) cane sugar or honey
Spices to taste
2 glasses of rum

1. Break the eggs into a large jug — beat well with honey and spice.

2. Heat the ale but do not boil. Pour onto the eggs beating well all the time. Heat all together and add the spirit. Best had before the fire on a cold winters night. Serves 6.

PRESERVING EGGS

PICKLED EGGS

Hard boil the eggs and store in vinegar. Malt vinegar will turn the eggs brown, so use spirit vinegar which will preserve their whiteness.

PRESERVING EGGS

Unless you keep hens or have a ready supply of cheap eggs there is little point in preserving them. However it used to be common practice and this is how it was done.

1. Brush the egg with clarified butter, molten wax or gum arabic, and store in a cool place with the pointed end down.

2. Store immersed in a bucket or jar containing a solution of waterglass or lime.

Eggs for preservation should be very fresh and be cleaned with a dry abrasive pad rather than washing.

WHAT TO DO WITH YOUR EGG SHELLS

If you keep hens, the shells can be dried, crushed up, and fed back to them, providing calcium for new egg shells. (Hens will also need additional calcium in the form of crushed oyster shell.)

Crushed egg shell also makes excellent collage material and can be glued onto paper or card and painted to give a beautiful scaly texture.

A few onion skins added to the pan when boiling eggs will turn their shells a rich yellow. Varying the amount of onion skins can produce a colour range from pale yellow to burnt orange. Spinach will colour shells green or brown and fruits such as blackberries and raspberries will give red and purple shades.

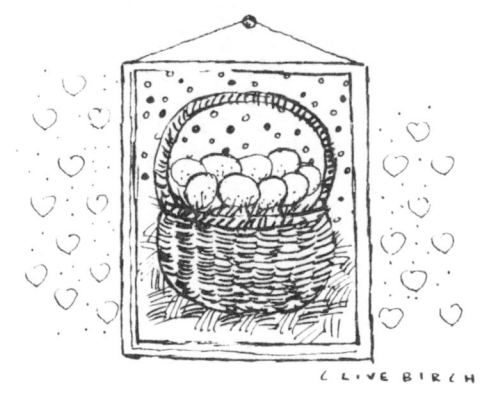

CLIVE BIRCH

INDEX